Bumblebee Bumblebee

by
Laura Becklar
illustrated by
Ann Murray

To my husband, children, and parents,
who were my inspiration.
And a special thank you to Katie Seifert,
Aimee Wendland, Marcia Moore, and Ann Murray
for their advice and support. LB

To Rick Murray.
And to our forever friends, the bees. ~ AM

• • • • •

The illustrations in this book were created using watercolor dyes, synthetic bristle brushes, micron pens, and digital painting. Recycled materials were used for the initial sketches.

Dear Parents,

The love of reading is a practice that begins at a very young age. From the time we are born, we instinctively love to hear and respond to the human voice. It is important to combine this interest with reading. This is a rhyming story that helps teach small children body parts. As you read, you will find that your child will become excited when they hear a word like "soot" because they will anticipate the rhyme scheme and start to hide their "foot" before you read that word.

Bumblebee Bumblebee is intended to create interaction between you and your child. First, create a loving, warm environment by having your child sit on your lap. Use inflection and excitement in your voice for added enjoyment and better comprehension. Then, the fun begins. Each time the bumblebee is going after a body part, be ready to tickle! I hope you and your child have hours of enjoyment as I have had with my own children.

Reading this book is a great way to bond with your child, while teaching them simple parts of the body in a fun way. Enjoy creating wonderful memories with your family.

Sincerely,

Laura Becklar, Author

It is a beautiful, sunny day.
With my friends, I want to play.

Out in the field,
down by the lake...

and on the farm,
oh what fun we will make!

There is one thing that
I hope not to see...

and that is a
busy little bumblebee.

Bumblebee, bumblebee
came from the farm...

he is going to get Kelly
right under the arm.

Bumblebee, bumblebee
came from the chair...

he is going to get Hannah
right in the hair.
(I do declare!)

Bumblebee, bumblebee
came from the hose...

he is going to get John
right in the nose.

Bumblebee, bumblebee
came from the soot...

he just might get Emily
right in the foot.

Bumblebee, bumblebee
flying with twirls and dips...

he is going to get Rusty
right on the hip.

Bumblebee, bumblebee
came from the deck...

he is going to get Alisa
right in the neck.

Bumblebee, bumblebee
came from the sand...

he is going to get Mary
right in the hand.

Bumblebee, bumblebee
came from the tree...

he is going to get Tyler
right in the knee.

Bumblebee, bumblebee
came from the bin...

he is going to get Ryan
right under the chin.

Bumblebee, bumblebee
I sure can hear...

that you're going to get Leah
behind the ear.

Bumblebee, bumblebee
came from down the road a mile.

and chased and chased
my poor friend Kyle.

Bumblebee, bumblebee
I would like to beg...

please don't get me
on the leg.

Bumblebee, bumblebee
you are cute I can see,

but could you please fly
away home and let us be!

Made in the USA
Columbia, SC
01 April 2019